How to Eradicate Bullying

Ronald W. Holmes, Ph.D.

Publisher, The Holmes Education Post, LLC

"An Education Focused Internet Newspaper"

authorHOUSE®

AuthorHouse™
1663 Liberty Drive
Bloomington, IN 47403
www.authorhouse.com
Phone: 1 (800) 839-8640

Published by AuthorHouse   08/06/2015

ISBN: 978-1-5049-2746-8 (sc)
ISBN: 978-1-5049-2745-1 (e)

Library of Congress Control Number: 2015912645

Print information available on the last page.

Table of Contents

ACKNOWLEDGEMENT

In writing this book, "How to Eradicate Bullying," I was concerned about the number of students who are bullied in school particularly on the elementary and middle school levels. I was also concerned about the negative impact bullying has on the victims and families.

Bullying is a serious and dangerous act, so schools must engage in research-based solutions to protect the safety and livelihood of their students. These solutions must incorporate anti-bullying policies, procedures and laws earmarked to address bullying in schools and prohibit discrimination and harassment based on race, color, national origin, sex, disability and religion.

Considering the time, energy and commitment it takes to write a book, I would like to thank my wife, Constance C. Holmes, for being the editor for it. Her continued dedication and unwavering support to my publications and service to public education is greatly appreciated.

DEDICATION

This book is dedicated to all the innocent victims of bullies and parents who have lost their loved ones due to bullying and other forms of violence in our schools.

It is my hope that this book will serve as a vehicle to improve public education and contribute to the eradication of bullying in the U.S. and abroad.

FOREWORD

Each day, an alarming number of students are either dropping out of school or afraid to go to school because of their bullies or perpetrators. According to the U.S. Department of Education, bullying is defined as "unwanted, aggressive, repetitive behavior that involves a real or perceived power imbalance" (DINatale, 2014). The bullying of today is quite different from the bullying of the past. As I recall during childhood, the perpetrator would not only instigate bullying but would also coordinate a scene for it to happen. In my day, the bully would get two guys to a scene, stand in the middle of the two guys and excite the conflict by saying, "the "baddest man, hit my hand." One of the guys would hit his hand and then the guys would start tussling. Once the brawl was done, the guys would dust themselves off and embrace each other like nothing had even happen.

In this era, however, bullying is at another level. It is not just a part of "growing up" as cited by President Obama at a White House's Conference on Bullying Prevention. It is the number one problem in schools according to Kaiser Family Foundation. Students are facing a high level of depression and anxiety when they are bullied verbally, physically and electronically. In fact, two-third of the students who attempted or completed shootings in America's schools were bullied according to the Secret Service as reported in Behavioral Management (Holmes, 2011).

Although there is no single factor why students are being bullied or bullying others, it is critical that we understand some risk factors of students' bullied or bullying others in the school, home and community. Research by StopBullying.gov (SBG) notes that some groups such as gay, lesbian, bisexual, youth with disabilities and socially isolated youth might have an increased risk of being bullied by their perpetrators. SBG distinguishes respectively, between students who are at risk of being bullied and more likely to bully others. The victim might be perceived as different from their peers whereas the perpetrator might have a propensity to dominate their peers.

Therefore, it is imperative that schools learn proactive ways to counteract bullying. According to The Institute on Family and Neighborhood, bullying might lead to other delinquent behaviors such as shoplifting, vandalism, truancy and constant drug use. It might contribute to a negative learning environment, cause short-term problems for victims such as anxiety and depression. It may also leave long-term scars on the victims such as depression and low self-esteem.

A well-known childhood rhyme from the past was, "Sticks and stone may break my bones, but words will never hurt me. In today's world, words and pictures may actually harm students psychologically if they are used in the form of sexting and cyber bullying. At the same time, an alarming number of students are being bullied physically.

Whether bullying occurs in the school, home and community, it is time to eradicate bullying in order to protect the safety and livelihood of children. This book provides research-based solutions to end this bully epidemic.

INTRODUCTION

Bullying is "when a student is exposed, repeatedly and over time to negative actions on the part of one or more students and he or she has difficulty defending himself or herself" (Olweus cited in Wood, 2013). Bullying is a serious epidemic in American schools. Bullying might come in the form of direct bullying such as physical or verbal aggressions and indirect or relational bullying such as cyber bullying or sexting. It can occur before, during or after school. Physical aggression might include assaulting, kicking, hitting and destroying physical property. Verbal aggression might include teasing, taunting, name calling, making threats and spreading rumors. Relational aggression might include staring deliberately at someone, using threatening or offensive gestures towards the person and leaving hurtful messages on electronic devices.

According to President Barrack Obama, "a third of middle school and high school students have reported being bullied during the school year." These incidents include teasing, shoving, pushing, spitting or tripping due to differences in their race, clothes, disability or sexual orientation. Bullies are causing nearly 160,000 students to be absent daily from school and 1.2 million to dropout of school annually according to the National Education Association.

In a national iSAFE study of fourth to eight graders, 42 percent of bullying victims suffered the impact of cyber bullying through electronic devices such as sexting or using the cell phones and Internet. Cyber bullying is when a child, preteen or teen is tormented, threatened, harassed, humiliated, embarrassed or otherwise targeted by another child, preteen or teen using the Internet, interactive and digital technologies or mobile phones. In many instances, these inappropriate acts are coordinated before students enter the school buildings.

Sexting is sending sexually explicit photos, videos or messages electronically from the cell phones. According to a survey conducted by The Associated Press, "more than one-in-four teenagers have sexted in some formed.

Thirty percent of all respondents said they had been involved in sexting. Seventy percent of respondents 14–24 years old said that somebody had sent them nude pictures or videos of themselves." It is easy for sexting to turn into bullying which has legal ramification.

In a typical scenario described by a law official to a group of high school students in Western Massachusetts, the following is how sexting presents problems for students: a female student agrees to text a nude picture of herself to a boyfriend as result of pressure from him. When the relationship ends, the boyfriend forwards the picture to other friends who may forward the picture to additional friends. The girl is harassed, bullied and embarrassed by the time the picture has circulated through her school. Consequently, the boyfriend and other parties could be charged with a felony, assessed fines and incarcerated if convicted. They could also be registered as a sex offender if the victim's age is under 18.

While there are 49 states with anti-bullying laws (See Figure 1), it is important that stakeholders such as parents and teachers recognize the signs of a child being bullied or being a bully respectively such as being afraid to go to school and becoming increasingly frustrated in school (Bullying Statistics, 2013). Other examples might include the victim's grades declining and the perpetrator's constantly referred to the school administrator for discipline (SBG).

Figure 1.
Anti-Bullying Laws in U.S. States

State / Enactment Date		
Georgia 1999	Virginia 2005	Utah 2008
New Hampshire 2000	Texas 2005	Florida 2008
Colorado 2001	Tennessee 2005	North Carolina 2009
Louisiana 2001	Maine 2005	Wyoming 2009
Mississippi 2001	Nevada 2005	Alabama 2009
Oregon 2001	Idaho 2006	Massachusetts 2010
West Virginia 2001	South Carolina 2006	Wisconsin 2010
Connecticut 2002	Alaska 2006	New York 2010
New Jersey 2002	New Mexico 2006	Missouri 2010
Oklahoma 2002	Delaware 2007	North Dakota 2011
Washington 2002	Iowa 2007	Hawaii 2011
Arkansas 2003	Illinois 2007	Michigan 2011
California 2003	Kansas 2007	South Dakota 2012
Rhode Island 2003	Minnesota 2007	
Vermont 2004	Ohio 2007	
Arizona 2005	Pennsylvania 2007	
Indiana 2005	Nebraska 2008	
Maryland 2005	Kentucky 2008	

State with no Anti-Bullying Law:
Montana

Similar to bullying, there are 44 states with anti-hazing laws (See Figure 2). Hazing comprises of "any activity expected of someone joining a group that humiliates, degrades, abuses or endangers regardless of the person's willingness to participate" in the activity. The activity is normally affiliated with an individual being physically and psychologically abused, depriving of sleep, carrying unwarranted objects, consuming alcohol, participating in sexual acts and paddling (Nuwer cited in Chang 2011). Hazing activity can occur on or off campus of educational institutions, by an individual alone or acting with others for the purpose of pledging, being initiated into, affiliating with holding office in an organization or maintaining membership in an organization.

Figure 2.
Anti-Hazing Laws in U.S. States

State / Enactment Date		
Illinois 1901	Massachusetts 1985	New Hampshire 1993
Rhode Island 1909	Kansas 1986	Washington (State) 1993
North Carolina 1913	Kentucky 1986	Nebraska 1994
Louisiana 1920	Pennsylvania 1986	North Dakota 1995
Michigan 1931	Missouri 1987	Tennessee 1995
Virginia 1975	South Carolina 1987	Texas 1995
California 1976	Connecticut 1988	West Virginia 1995
Indiana 1976	Georgia 1988	Minnesota 1997
New Jersey 1980	Iowa 1989	Colorado 1999
Alabama 1981	Maine 1989	Nevada 1999
Ohio 1982	Utah 1989	Vermont 1999
Arkansas 1983	Mississippi 1990	Arizona 2001
New York 1983	Oklahoma 1990	Florida 2002
Oregon 1983	Idaho 1991	Maryland 2002
Wisconsin 1983	Delaware 1992	

States with no Anti-Hazing Law:
Alaska
Hawaii
Montana
New Mexico
South Dakota
Wyoming

Whether it is direct bullying, indirect bullying or hazing, they all may have the same psychological and physical effect on students such as low self-esteem, poor performance in school, severe illness and death. Schools are confronted with these dangerous acts committed by perpetrators throughout the U.S. They must employ research-based interventions to eradicate bullying.

As a result, this book discusses a nine-step model to eradicate bullying and other forms of harassment, intimidation and bigotry from the school culture. This book provides a model (See Figure 3) for better understanding and reinforcement of the strategies to eradicate bullying from the educational setting using the acronym, "ERADICATE."

Figure 3.

Nine-Step Model

E	Educate students, parents and teachers on policies, procedures and laws on bullying
R	Review routinely policies, procedures and laws on bullying
A	Address and ensure all students and teachers are accountable to policies, procedure and laws on bullying
D	Discuss the characteristics of the Bully, Victim, Bully-victim and Bystander; and the Signs of Bullying
I	Implement activities in educational setting on anti-bullying prevention strategies
C	Communicate the impact of bullying
A	Adopt best practices on eradicating bullying
T	Teach anti-bullying curriculum in educational setting
E	Evaluate periodically anti-bullying prevention strategies in educational setting

Defining Bullying

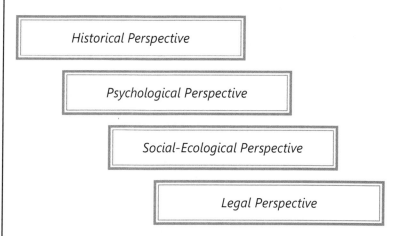

With bullying being interwoven in American society and constantly occurring in the community and schools, we must clearly understand the meaning of bullying from a historical, psychological, social-ecological and legal perspective. We must recognize characteristics and signs of bullying and learn appropriate steps for stopping it.

Historical Perspective

In this century, bullying has increasingly become a major societal problem as reported in the media. It may come in the form of direct bullying such as physical or verbal aggressions and indirect bullying or relational aggression such as cyber bullying or sexting. In the U.S., for example, the Columbine High School massacre in Colorado in 1999, brought attention to this epidemic. At that time, it was perhaps one of the most deadly school shootings in America where two students killed twelve classmates, a teacher and wounded twenty-four others before killing themselves. Over a year, these students strategically planned their retaliation against their schoolmates who had bullied them (Raywid cited in Fegenbush 2010).

Prior to this incident and due to the request for parental consent in the U.S., little or no research was done about bullying except in other countries such as Australia and Europe. In the 1970s, Dan Olweus considered the founding father of bullying, published a book called the Aggression in the Schools: Bullies and Whipping Boys in 1973 in Scandinavia and in 1978 in the U.S. After a 1983 suicide-related death of three adolescent boys severely bullied by their perpetrators in Norway, Norwegian officials initiated a national campaign against bullying in Norwegian schools. Olweus, a native of Norway, developed the first Olweus Bullying Prevention Program (OBPP) to address school bullying with proactive and reactive measures on the school, class and individual levels utilizing a set of criteria/recommendations for each level such as a questionnaire survey, role playing and change of class. The OBPP is designed in order that school stakeholders such as teachers, staff and administrators are provided responsibility to introduce and implement the anti-bullying program. It is the most used program in the world. Please see Figure 4 as published in Fegenbush (2010).

As a part of his research, Olweus in 1987 obtained data from 140,000 students in 715 Norwegian schools whereas 15% were involved in bullying of some type, 94% were classified as victims and 6% were classified as bullies. While the definitions of bullying varies in studies, Olweus defined bullying as "when a student is exposed, repeatedly and over time, to negative actions on the part of one or more students and he or she has difficulty defending himself or herself" (Olweus cited in Wood, 2013).

With a basis for understanding this bullying phenomenon, Olweus' research caught on in other countries in the 1980s and 1990s, and a plethora of research on bullying was studied by American researchers near 2001, said Fegenbush. In 2001, for instance, a national study was conducted in the U.S. of 15,686 sixth through tenth graders about bullying. Approximately 29.9% of the students reported moderate to frequent involvement in bullying, 13% identified themselves as bullies, 10.6% identified themselves as victims and 6.3% identified themselves as bully-victims according to Espelage & Swearer (cited in Wood 2013).

In 2010, the Josephson Institute of Ethics conducted a large study in the U.S. regarding the attitudes of 43,321 high schools students. From this study, 50% of the students admitted they had bullied a person in the previous year, and 47% indicated they were bullied, taunted or teased in a way that frustrated them in the previous year also (Josephson Institute of Ethics cited in Wood 2013).

Thus, it is time to eradicate bullying and other forms of harassment, intimidation and bigotry from the school culture. Students should not feel unsafe in school and jeopardized of a quality education.

Figure 4.
Components of Olweus' Bullying Intervention Program

Level of Implementation	Criteria/Recommendations
Measures at the School Level	Questionnaire Survey School conference day on bully/victim problems Better supervision during recess and lunch time Contact telephone Meeting staff-parents Teacher groups for the development of the social milieu of the school Parent circles
Measure at the Class Level	Class rules against bullying: clarification, praise and sanctions Regular class meetings Role playing, literature, cooperative learning Common positive class activities Class meeting teacher – parent/children
Measures at the Individual	Serious talks with bullies and victims Serious talks with parents of involved students Teacher and parent use of imagination Help from "neutral" student Help and support for parents of bullies and victims Change of class or school

In order to understand human development, psychologist Urie Bronfenbrenner proposed in 1979 a theory of ecological-systems. This system is comprised of "five socially organized subsystems that guide human growth and development" through a child's social relationships and surrounding environment. They include microsystem, mesosystem, exosystem, macrosystem and chronosystem. The microsystem relates to the interaction a child has with his immediate environment such as school, home, daycare, work, peers, teachers or family members. For example, a child who has a nourishing home with parents and siblings, attends a safe school with supportive teachers and peers can benefit positively from this type of climate.

The mesosytem comprises of the interactions between the different components of a child's microsystem and on how the environments impacts his or her development. One example would be the relationship between the child's guardian and teacher. For example, a child's parent who attends Parent Teacher Student Association meetings regularly and volunteers in the child's classroom and school activities can have a positive impact on the child's development because the different components of the microsystem are working harmoniously together.

The exosystem consists of environments that do not encompass the child in an active role but still have an impact on him or her. For example, a child's parent who gets a raise or fired from a job can have a deleterious influence on the child although the child did not have anything to do with the employer's decision.

The macrosystem relates to the cultural environments in which a child resides, as well as the influences from all of the systems (microsystem, mesosystem and exosystems) have on the individual. For instance, a child's living environment in a particular city, state or country can be different from another child and, subsequently, have a positive or negative influence on the individual's development. The chronosystem relates to the changes in the characteristics of a child over time, as well as the environment where the individual resides. For example, a parent's divorce and change in residency from the other spouse can have a negative impact on a child's behavior for a certain period of time.

Thus, a close examination of the ecological systems theory proposed by psychologist Bronfenbrenner, provides research to help understand why people behave differently in one setting versus another environment such as the home, school, and work (Bronfenbrenner cited in Wood, 2013). School leaders should be knowledgeable of these subsystems that guide human growth and development to improve the learning process.

Sociological-Ecological Perspective

Drawing on Bronfenbrenner's research on the five socially organized subsystems that guide human growth and development through a child's social relationships and surrounding environment, Swearer and Espelage in 2004 established a social-ecological framework of bullying among youth. Components of the framework include culture, community, school, peers, family, bully, bully-victim, victim, and bystander (See Figure 5). Swearer and Espelage highlight that bullying does not occur in isolation since the relationships across family, peer, school, and community contexts will impact the engagement or non-engagement in bullying and victimization behaviors. Since bullying is a "complex phenomenon with multiple causal factors and outcomes," they advocate, and affirmed by other researchers, that intervention programs on bullying will be most effective if the programs target multiple environments such as the home, community and school (Swearer and Espelage cited in Wood, 2013).

Figure 5.
A Social-ecological framework of bullying among youth.

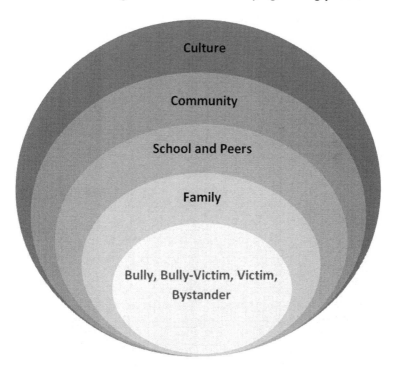

Bullying is an epidemic in American schools resulting in 49 states to adopt anti-bullying laws. It impacts people of all races, genders, ages, religions and class. When schools are confronted with challenges of students being bullied by their perpetrators, this can lead to potential lawsuits on the basis of Title VI, IX, Section 504 of the Rehabilitation Act of 1973, and Title II of the Americans with Disabilities Act of 1990. Depending on the court cases, schools may be forced to develop, implement and or expand their policies and procedures, as well as take appropriate measures to prevent and respond to bullying incidents.

For effective practices, it is critical that schools appoint an anti-bullying coordinator, train their faculty and staff on anti-bullying preventions, investigate thoroughly bullying incidents and have a communication plan for informing all stakeholders such as parents of anti-bullying prevention activities and the consequences of bullying acts.

Liability issues pertaining to students being bullied or hazed through events such as extra-curricular activities can range from schools being negligent for lack of supervision and failure to provide a reasonable duty of care for the victims. Other liability issues can include failure of schools to provide a safe environment, failure to report an incident to the authority (knowingly or unknowingly), failure to educate, supervise and evaluate school stakeholders (students, faculty members, etc.), failure to develop and implement policies and procedures and failure to properly enforce anti-bullying laws.

While there are no perfect educational institutions, it is essential that schools take proactive steps to effectively address bullying in their settings. Courts are bombarded with legal cases and decisions to determine if there were a "duty of care" between student victims of bullying and educational institutions, as well as if the institutions are "deliberately indifferent" to the harassment that is so severe, pervasive, and objectively offensive that it effectively inhibits the student victims' access to an educational benefit or opportunity.

Therefore, schools must employ appropriate measures to prevent and respond to bullying incidents on their campuses including students participating in school sponsored activities, students riding school provided transportation and students using school-owned technology. They must adopt policies, procedures and laws that prohibit the harassment, intimidation and bullying (HIB) of their students. According to the U.S. Department of Education, a number of states are leaders in providing bullying policies such as Georgia, Florida, Kansas and Massachusetts, which includes a provision to provide training to staff members and help them prevent, identify and respond to bullying in the educational setting. For understanding of why schools must adopt policies, procedures and laws to prohibit HIB, Figure 6 provides some examples of legal cases on bullying.

Figure 6.
Legal Cases

In the 2007, L.W. v. Tom River Regional Board of Education case, the New Jersey Supreme Court established that a school district can be held liable when the district fails to act reasonably to end a student-on student harassment complaint on the basis of sexual orientation that creates a hostile educational environment under the Law Against Discrimination for student-on-student harassment.

In the 2011 T.K. and S.K. v. New York City Department of Education case, the federal district court applied a broad standard of liability to the New York public schools, that a female student with disability had stated a valid claim of being denied a free appropriate public education under the federal Individuals with Disabilities Education Act, as result of school officials' failure to remedy student-on-student bullying and harassment based on the victim's disability. Using a 2010 "Dear Colleague Letter " to schools as reference, the federal district court concluded that schools take immediate and appropriate action when in response to bullying incidents that might impede with a special education student's ability to receive an appropriate education.

In the 2011 (Ohio Court of Appeal) Golden v. Milford Exempted Village School District case, involved a sexual aggressor attack on a freshman high school student by several teammates while waiting to be transported on a school-sponsored bus to basketball practice without adult supervision. Once the school district learned of the complaint, it conducted an investigation. Both the parent and student victim filed suit against the basketball coach and school district regarding negligent supervision and civil hazing. The Court of appeal ruled that the acts committed were bullying instead of hazing, and that the basketball coach did not act in a willful manner that would lead to negligence or liability.

How to Eradicate Bullying

Step I - Educate Stakeholders

Bullying is the number one problem in schools according to Kaiser Family Foundation. It is causing students to face a high level of depression and anxiety when they are bullied verbally, physically and electronically. Astoundingly, nearly 160,000 students are absent from school and 1.2 dropout of school annually due to their bullies according to the National Education Association. Additionally, two-third of the students who attempted or completed shootings in America's schools were bullied according to the Secret Service as reported in Behavioral Management.

To ensure the safety of individuals for all "protected classes," (race, ethnicity, gender, religion, disability, nationality and sexual orientation), we must educate all stakeholders such as students, parents, teachers, administrators and community representatives on the policies, procedures and laws for anti-bullying preventions. Students must know clearly what the policies, procedures and laws are regarding bullying in the educational setting. This information must be very transparent regardless of whether students are participating in extra-curricular activities, attending school sponsored field trips or engaging in other school activities.

In this millennium, children between ages eight and 18 spend an average of 53 hours a week using electronic media such as Facebook, Twitter, Myspace, cell phones and video games which leads to lower school grades and students being less happy, according to a study by Kaiser Family Foundation. Through bullying tactics such as sexting and cyberbullying, a third of middle school and high school students have reported being bullied during the school year.

At the 2013 Blueprint For Excellence National Conference in Walt Disney World Rosort, Florida, Dr. David Walsh, founder of Mind Positive Parenting indicated that "whatever the brain does a lot is what it gets good at doing." He also indicated that four out of five teens sleep with their cell phones near them, and 20 percent of babies born have some type of technology device. Realizing this, it is essential to teach children in this information age digital awareness to avoid overuse and misuse of technology such as sexting and cyberbullying.

Therefore, anti-bullying preventions information must be an essential part of the Student Code of Conduct and any extra-curricular activity in the academic setting. Along with the faculty sponsor reviewing the policies, procedures and laws with students on bullying for their respective activity, schools must create anti-bullying training including a campus 24-hour anonymous bullying hotline. Students must complete an assessment questionnaire after the training to prove their knowledge and understanding of bullying, as well as know whom to call if they have any concerns. Educational institutions that use a "whole school approach" to address bullying such as the Olweus Bullying Prevention Program, include all stakeholders in the school-wide bullying prevention program.

In addition to completing the assessment questionnaire, students must complete a class assignment such as an essay on bullying which coincide with most states to offer students some type of educational offering on bullying (McCormac, 2015). They must also participate in a school or community service project regarding anti-bullying preventions before participating in a school activity or attending a school sponsored fieldtrip. We have to educate all stakeholders such as students on bullying to ensure that they fully understand the seriousness of the matter. With these requirements intact combined with students maintaining good academic standing and behavior, our expectation for student safety and participation in extra-curricular activities and school sponsored fieldtrips will be enhanced and substantiated by interventions as a viable means to eradicate bullying. Figure 7 provides a sample letter for schools to use to educate student stakeholders, support the Student Code of Conduct and provide proof of anti-bullying prevention compliance.

Jane S. Doe Public School
Office of Administration
3000 Tammy Street East, Lake City, Fla. 32055

Anti-Bullying Prevention Policy Compliance

(**Educate Students**)

This letter confirms that I have read, fully understand and completed the following requirements of the Jane S. Doe Public School Anti-Bullying Prevention Policy.

Specifically, I have completed the Online Bullying Training, assessment questionnaire and know how to report bullying acts anonymously through the campus 24-hour hotline.

Also, I have completed both a class assignment regarding the anti-bullying training and the required community service project regarding anti-bullying prevention.

Bullying Definition
Bullying is defined as "when a student is exposed, repeatedly and over time, to negative actions on the part of one or more students and he or she has difficulty defending himself or herself."

Florida Bullying Law
"Bullying means systematically and chronically inflicting physical hurt or psychological distress on one or more students and may involve: teasing; social exclusion; threat; intimidation; stalking; physical violence; theft; sexual or racial harassment; public humiliation; or destruction of property."

Online Bullying Training
Provides training on the policies, procedures and laws, etc. regarding anti-bullying prevention at Jane S. Doe Public School.

| *An open door to your future.* | *www.janesdoepublicschool.com* |

Jane S. Doe Public School

Office of Administration
3000 Tammy Street East, Lake City, Fla. 32055

Anti-Bullying Prevention Policy Compliance

(**Educate Students** – *cont'd*)

Assessment Questionnaire
Provides an assessment of the Online Bullying Training at Jane S. Doe Public School for reinforcement of anti-bullying prevention.

Campus 24-hour Bullying Hotline
Affords an opportunity for students to report bullying anonymously at Jane S. Doe Public School.

Class Assignment
Provides a class assignment such as an essay to show student proof of understanding anti-bullying prevention before participating in any extra-curricular activities and school sponsored fieldtrips at Jane S. Doe Public School.

Community Service Project
Provides a community service project of student proof of anti-bullying prevention before participating in any extra-curricular activities and school-sponsored fieldtrips at Jane S. Doe Public School.

Office of Administration

_____
Student's Name (Print)

_____
Student's Signature

_____
School Officials' Signature

_____
Date

_____
Date

An open door to your future. | *www.janesdoepublicschool.com*

Step II - Review Policies, Procedures and Laws

Having policies, procedures and laws are very important, but reviewing them are just as important. To eradicate bullying, we must routinely review the policies, procedures and laws on anti-bullying preventions with all stakeholders such as students, faculty members and parents at the school. In Step I of the model, we discussed how to eradicate bullying through the involvement of students. In Step II of the model, we provide examples of how to eradicate bullying through the involvement of parent stakeholders.

Bullying is a major problem for students in America's schools, yet many parents fail to talk to their children about the matter according to Kaiser Family Foundation. Therefore, schools must use social media, newsletters, websites, special events and online bullying training to review and discuss periodically the policies, procedures and laws on anti-bullying preventions. Through social media such as Facebook and Twitter, this will give parents an opportunity to periodically review information on bullying and participate in dialogue for improved knowledge and understanding. Also, through newsletters, websites, special events and online bullying training, this will give parents an opportunity to review pertinent information on bullying and participate in anti-bullying prevention programs in the school setting. Ultimately, this will provide a paper trail of interventions to eradicate bullying from the school culture. Figure 8 provides a sample newsletter to parents illustrating Jane S. Doe Public School's approach to review the policies, procedures and laws of anti-bullying preventions. This same letter can be tailored for faculty, teachers and staff members since they, staff members such as bus drivers, food service and security workers, receive the least amount of training on anti-bullying prevention strategies. With inadequate training, this leads to many staff members perceiving bullying differently from students and not sufficiently responding to bullying complaints. Subsequently, this leads to many students being less inclined to report bullying incidents to them (National Education Association, 2010).

Jane S. Doe Public School

Office of Administration
3000 Tammy Street East, Lake City, Fla. 32055

Anti-Bullying Prevention Policy Compliance
(Review Policies, Procedures and Laws - PPL)

Welcome parents to the 2015 – 2016 academic year! This newsletter focuses on the approaches we are using to promote zero tolerance of bullying at Jane S. Doe Public School (JSDPS).

These strategies include our social media campaign, monthly newsletter, special events and online bullying training:

SOCIAL MEDIA	*WEBSITE*	*ONLINE BULLYING TRAINING*
We provide parents an opportunity to follow us on Twitter at Jane S. Doe Public School to gain the latest information on anti-bullying preventions.	We have a Bullying website to display information, review and discuss periodically the policies, procedures and laws on anti-bullying preventions.	We require students to complete the Online Bullying Training at Jane S. Doe Public School before they can participate in any extra-curricular activities and attend any school fieldtrips.
NEWSLETTER	*SPECIAL EVENTS*	We encourage parents to complete the bullying training to review the PPL on anti-bullying preventions.
We will post a monthly newsletter on our website at JSDPS to reiterate the PPL regarding anti-bullying preventions.	We will promote and participate in special events on the campus of JSDPS to review the PPL regarding anti-bullying preventions.	We enlist parents to help us reinforce the expectation of anti-bullying preventions to all stakeholders at the school.

Again, we welcome parents to this academic year. Your active involvement is greatly appreciated

An open door to your future.	*www.janesdoepublicschool.com*

Step III - Address Accountability

People drive their automobiles everyday with the understanding of the laws and consequences for breaking the laws. When they break the laws by speeding, reckless driving or driving under the influence of alcohol, they are held accountable. This might include having to attend a driver's education class, suspension or loss of their driver's license. In the same manner, we must address and ensure that all stakeholders at the school such as teachers are held accountable for the policies, procedures and laws on anti-bullying preventions.

In the previous two steps of the model, we noted the need to educate stakeholders and review policies, procedures and laws about bullying respectively through the involvement of students and parents. In Step III, we provide examples of how to eradicate bullying through the involvement of faculty members such as teachers. For example, schools must use these stakeholders to address accountability through transparency or evidence such as lesson plans, bulletin boards, newsletters, websites, social media and online bullying training.

In addition to faculty members such as teachers receiving anti-bullying training, school officials must require that teachers make sure the policies, procedures and laws on anti-bulling preventions are a part of their course syllabi. For accountability, school officials can assess evidence of this being communicated accordingly through visiting and communicating with teachers in their classrooms, reviewing department chairs' accountability folders and/or posting of syllabi on schools' websites. Just as drivers of automobiles are held accountable for driving safely, teachers must be held accountable for communicating information so the message about anti-bullying prevention is reinforced and taken seriously throughout the educational environment. Figure 9 provides a sample of an abbreviated teacher course syllabus to show or address accountability of bullying through transparency.

Furthermore, school boards must hold school leaders such as administrators accountable for ensuring that they are taking proactive means to address accountability regarding anti-bullying preventions, as well as investigating fully incidents of bullying allegations at the highest level possible. Courts are bombarded with legal cases and decisions to determine if there were a "duty of care" between student victims of bullying and educational institutions, as well as if the institutions are "deliberately indifferent" to the harassment that is so severe, pervasive, and objectively offensive that it effectively inhibits the student victims' access to an educational benefit or opportunity. Figure 6 provides examples of some legal cases on bullying as previously mentioned.

Jane S. Doe Public School

Office of Administration
3000 Tammy Street East, Lake City, Fla. 32055

Reading Prep Course Syllabus
Fall 2015

Anti-Bullying Prevention Policy Compliance
(Address Accountability)

Course Description
The purpose of this course is to provide test-taking strategies to prepare students for the reading portion of the state exam.

Course Topic
Reading Comprehension Skills

School Rules & Expectations

Understand that bullying is defined as "when a student is exposed, repeatedly and over time, to negative actions on the part of one or more students and he or she has difficulty defending himself or herself."

Understand that there are 49 states with anti-bullying laws. In Florida, for instance, "Bullying means systematically and chronically inflicting physical hurt or psychological distress on one or more students and may involve: teasing; social exclusion; threat; intimidation; stalking; physical violence; theft; sexual or racial harassment; public humiliation; or destruction of property."

I have read, fully understand and agree to Jane S. Doe Public School's anti-bullying prevention policy.

_____
Student's Name (Print)

_____

_____
Student's Signature

_____
Date

21

Step IV – Discuss the Characteristics of the Bully, Victim, Bully-victim and Bystander; and the Signs of Bullying

In Step IV, we discuss the characteristics of the bully, victim, bully-victim and bystander. We also discuss the signs of bullying. The bully, for instance, uses power to intimidate or harm a person who is weaker, appears to be more prevalent in boys than girls and more associated with younger children than older children. The victim is the target of the bullying and receives repeated coercive behavior from the bully. The bully-victim is an individual who bully others, a victim of the bully and exuberates a high level of depression and aggression. The bystander is the observer or onlooker of the bullying incident and may watch the bullying and not do anything, influence the bullying through gestures and comments or intervene to help the victim from the bully (Wood, 2013).

During my childhood era, the bully would get two guys to a scene, stand in the middle of the two guys and excite the conflict by saying, "the baddest man, hit my hand." One of the guys would hit the bully's hand and then the guys would start tussling. Once the brawl was done, the guys would dust themselves off and embrace each other like nothing had ever happen. On a rare occasion, the bully would target one particular victim and make the person run errands for him or demand things such as food from the victim's home. The bully would also take the victim's position in a sporting event such as baseball, if he came late to the event, at the time players were selected for each team.

Thus, it is important that school stakeholders such as parents and teachers recognize the signs of a child being bullied or being a bully. According to Bullying Statistics' website, stakeholders should notice the child presumed as being bullied if the child (1) becomes withdrawn from activities; (2) possesses fear upon going to school; (3) shows increasing symbols of depression; (4) shows a decline in academic achievement; (5) interacts with other children in fear; (6) losses self-confidence in himself or herself; (7) provides evidence of physical scars and (8) losses interest in attending school.

Additionally, Stopbullying.gov provides information on the signs of a child being bullied or being a bully. A number of signs that might reveal a bullying problem if a child has (1) unjustifiable injuries; (2) lost of personal property such as clothes and electronics; (3) constant illnesses such as stomach pain and headaches; (4) severe change in eating habits or lack of eating meals as scheduled; (5) constant nightmares or sleeping difficulties (6) decrease in grades, interest in class assignments or desire to attend school; (7) loss of personal friends and self esteem; (8) seen different in their appearance from their peers and (9) talk about hurting or harming himself/herself physically.

As a child is being a bully to another child, stakeholders such as parents and teachers should notice the bully (1) views violence positively as a viable solution to most problems; (2) shows aggression toward elders and other children; (3) needs to control situations and dominate others; (4) becomes easily upset; (5) shows little sympathy to those who are being bullied or facing issues; and (6) prefers not to help stop bullying, according to research on Bullying Statistics.

Furthermore, a number of signs that might reveal a child is bullying others if the child: (1) becomes involved in verbal and physical fights; (2) has peers who bully other children; (3) becomes more aggressive toward others; (4) gets referred constantly to the administrator's office or assigned school detention; (5) encounters unsubstantiated extra cash or new accessories; (6) accuses others for their own problems; (7) declines to take responsibility for their wrongdoing; (8) worries about their popularity and image and (9) has little or no parental support or has conflicting issues in the home or community.

Schools must become aware of these characteristics of bullying, as well as the signs of bullying. The information (characteristics and signs of bullying) relates directly to Bronfenbrenner's five socially organized subsystems (microsystem, mesosystem, exosystem, macrosystem and chronosystem) that guide human growth and development through a child's social relationships and surrounding environment. The information must become an integral part of schools anti-bullying prevention programs in order to maintain an educational setting that is safe and conducive to learning.

Step V - Implement Activities

It is written that "we learn best by doing." To eradicate bullying from our school, we must implement activities that bring attention to bullying. In the first three steps of the model, we noted the need to educate stakeholders, review policies, procedures and laws and address accountability about bullying respectively through the involvement of faculty members such as teachers. In the fourth step of the model, we discussed the characteristics and signs of bullying. In Step V, we provide examples of how to eradicate bullying through the involvement of school and community organizations.

There are many school-wide bullying prevention programs in the U.S. and abroad designed to stop bullying in schools. One notable program used throughout the World is the Olweus Bullying Prevention Program. As highlighted previously in Figure 4, the OBPP addresses school bullying with proactive and reactive measures on the school, class and individual levels. According to Fegenbush (2010), Olweus reported the impact of school acts of bullying utilizing the OBPP victim questionnaire of students who had participated in the program for 2.5 years. The survey results of participants pre-and post-tests revealed: (1) a "50% reduction in bullying behaviors; (2) a clear reduction in anti-social behaviors such as vandalism, fighting, and truancy; (3) an increased student satisfaction with school life," etc. This study was replicated in a study called Sheffield Project where students were administered pre-and post-test surveys. The survey results of participants corroborated with those of the OBPP such as, "a 40% reduction rate in student reporting acts of bullying."

As an example of Olweus' proactive measures at the class level, the San Francisco District Attorney George Gascón (DA) coupled with community partners, launched an annual 'Bye Bye Bullying' video contest for San Francisco middle and high school students which is the DA's office truancy initiative to keep students in school.

For this contest, during October's National Bullying Prevention Awareness Month, the DA enlisted students to create a 60 second video that addressed "Being Bully Free, Starts with Me" demonstrating how young people can intervene when faced with cyberbullying. The contest's submission period began October 6 and ended November 10. The students of the winning videos (first through third) were honored at a December celebration and featured on the San Francisco District Attorney's website. They also received prizes such as a gift card, Jawbone Jambox Classic and a signed baseball from the San Francisco Giants.

According to Gascón, "Cyberbullying continues to be a serious problem with nearly 70 percent of young people reporting seeing frequent bullying online. For the contest, we asked students to not only create thoughtful and innovative solutions to prevent cyberbullying, but to also consider their role in creating a bully free environment" (The Holmes Education Post, 2014).

Since bullying is an epedimic in today's society with numerous factors contributing to bullying acts, it is imperative that schools implement activities that bring attention to bullying. Researchers advocate that intervention programs on bullying will be most effective if they target mutiple environments such as the home, community and school (See Social-ecological framwork, Figure 5).

As we consistently implement these types of activities coupled with others strategically planned for the entire educational environment such as the National Bullying Prevention Month established by StompOutBullying.org and Pacer's National Bullying Prevention Center to promote the awareness and dangers of bullying, this will serve a strong means to eradicate bullying in schools.

Step VI - Communicate Impact

Bullying impacts the victims as well as their families. To eradicate bullying, we must understand the impact and communicate this impact has on the lives of citizens.

In Steps 1 – 5 of the model, we noted the need to educate stakeholders, review policies, procedures and laws, address accountability, discuss characteristics of bullying and their signs and prevent bullying through the involvement of school and community organizations. In Step VI, we communicate the impact of bullying through the documentary movie "Bully," by Lee Hirsch.

In "Bully," the public sees a compelling view of the effects of bullying. This movie depicts the tragedies of students who have been affected mentally and physically by their bullies, as well as the seriousness of the problem across ethnic, geographical and economic boundaries.

First, there is Alex, a timid 12-year old seventh grader from Sioux City, Iowa who was repeatedly threatened on the school bus, called offensive names such as "Fish Face" and punched by his perpetrators. To avoid making waves, Alex tells his concerned parents the classmates are "just messing with him." Second, there is Kelby, a 16-year old high school basketball star-athlete from Tuttle, Oklahoma. Kelby was ridiculed when she announced being a lesbian, called derogatory names such as "faggot" and faced bigotry by stakeholders at the school. Kelby was determined to remain in Tuttle despite her parents' wishes to leave the city to avoid the unnecessary and unwanted abuse by her bullies.

Third, there is Ja'Meya, a quiet 14-year old girl from Yazoo County, Mississippi who was repeatedly teased by her bullies on the school bus. Pushed to the brink, Ja'Meya took her mother's handgun on the school bus to stop her perpetrators. She was charged with multiple felony counts and placed in a juvenile detention facility. Fourth, there is the story of

17-year old Tyler from Murray County, Georgia who was overpowered by the bullying acts of classmates, indifferences of school officials and hanged himself in his parent's home. According to Tyler's father, David Long, "I knew he would be victimized at some point in time. He had a target on his back. Everybody knew that."

Finally, there is the story of Ty, an 11-year old from Perkins, Oklahoma who committed suicide as a result of bullying. His grief stricken parents, Kirk and Laura Smalley, are determined to prevent other children from been tormented from bullying and launched an anti-bullying organization called "Stand for the Silent." According to the father: "We are nobody and if it had been some politician's son, there would be a law tomorrow" (The Holmes Education Post, 2012).

If you have ever lost a loved one, particularly, a child to a tragedy, it is a feeling that can take your breath away, so to speak. Some people never get over it and others seek some level of peace by organizing civic activities to address the issue. The movie, "Bully" brings needed attention to this issue and calls for a nation to act.

Parents such as the Smalley's are calling on people across the nation to "Stand for the Silent" to end bullying and save children's lives. This campaign encourages children to become aware of the dangers of bullying and inform authorities when they see bullying occurring. With the alarming rate of kids being victimized by bullying, it is time that we all, "Stand for the Silent" and eliminate bullying from our culture.

Step VII – Adopt Best Practices

We must adopt best practices that are research-based to eradicate bullying from the educational environment. Bullying leads to the victims having low self-esteem, poor grades, mental health issues, loss of friends and interest in extra-curricular activities, as well as revenge on their perpetrators. In the resources section of this book, we highlight a number of organizations that are providing resources and intervention programs to address bullying in schools. Some of these organizations include: Anti-Bullying Alliance (http://www.anti-bullyingalliance.org.uk/); National Education Association (http://www.nea.org/home/neabullyfree.html); The Bullying Project (http://www.thebullyproject.com/; Olweus Bullying Prevention Program (htpp://www.violencepreventionworks.org/public/index.page), The Holmes Education Post (theholmeseducationpost.com) and Einestine Technology Services (www.einestinetechnology.com).

The Anti-Bullying Alliance is a coalition of organizations and individuals working together to stop bullying and create safe environments in which children and young people can live, grow, play and learn. The National Education Association is the nation's largest professional employee organization committed to advancing the cause of public education. NEA's 3 million members work at every level of education from pre-school to university graduate programs. The Bullying Project mission is to build a national movement to end bullying.

Since the release of Bully, the film has been screened to over a million kids, teachers, parents, and advocates. The Olweus Bullying Prevention Program is a whole-school approach model that addresses school bullying with proactive and reactive measures on the school, class and individual levels. OBPP is the most used program in the world, and it includes strategies to involve the parent and community in the whole-school approach model. The school stakeholders such as administrators, faculty and staff are responsible for the implementation of the program with the goal of improving student relations and making the educational climate safe and positive for learning (Fegenbush, 2010).

In addition to an Online National Anti-Hazing Curriculum designed to eradicate hazing from the institution's culture, The Holmes Education Post formed partnership with Einestine Technology Services and developed an Online National Anti-Bullying Curriculum to address the dangers of bullying in schools. This book serves as the reference guide for the online program. Using a whole-school approach, the objectives of the online program are to educate school stakeholders (students, parents, faculty members, etc.) on the policies, procedures and laws on anti-bullying preventions and provide an understanding of the negative effects of bullying. The online program can be adapted to fit any educational institution's brand and made available in multiple platforms including OSX, Android, Windows, as well as device agnostic (tablet, phone, laptop). Other features of the curriculum include: clear and colorful presentation; user friendly and very engaging; multiple choice questions with response explanations; test results of answer choices; passing percentage of performance; and easy to read and listen to information during the training.

Step VIII - Teach Anti-Bullying Curriculum

Bullying is an integral part of the American culture. It occurs "when a student is exposed, repeatedly and over time to negative actions on the part of one or more students and he or she has difficulty defending himself or herself" (Olweus cited in Wood, 2013). To eradicate bullying from the school culture, we must help students recognize and understand the seriousness and dangers of it. We must help students to better understand how to cope and prevent bullying whether it occurs in the classroom, on the street or through electronic means. Just as we teach English across the curriculum, we must teach anti-bullying prevention strategies across the curriculum that are research-oriented for students in the school setting.

In fact, this model must reflect a multi-disciplined approach that provides year-long training and activities to all parties (students, parents, faculty members, etc.) about the dangers of bullying. This type of whole-school approach model resembles programs such as Olweus Bullying Prevention Program and The Holmes Education Post/Einestine Technology Services (THEP/ETS) Online National Anti-Bullying Curriculum. The whole-school approach allows schools to involve the entire constituents associated with the educational environment since bullying is a systemic problem (Smith, Schneider, Smith & Ananiadou cited in Wood, 2013).

For THEP/EST online program, the training teaches students about the policies, procedures and laws on anti-bullying preventions; and ways to recognize and report bullying through means such as a parent, faculty member or 24-hour anonymous bullying hotline. The training also teaches students how to deal with bullying through interventions such as peer mediation and community service projects. For teachers, the training teaches ways to incorporate activities in the lessons such as essays on bullying preventions. For parents, the training teaches them about anti-bullying preventions that are in place at the school to protect their children from dangerous acts of bullying. The training also teaches parents how to recognize the characteristics and signs of bullying so they can immediately get help for their children. For school administrators, the training teaches them how to evaluate the effectiveness of activities on bullying preventions in the school setting.

As a supplement to this online program, it is important that school leaders build strong relationships with their students in the educational environment so that they become compelled to inform the authorities directly or anonymously of any form of bigotry or harassment confronting their safety, health or life. Having a positive learning environment where students and teachers are socially and intellectually interacting with each other can be helpful in the implementation and investigation of anti-bullying programming (Banks, 2011). An effective way to build positive relationships with students is through the Appreciative Advising framework (AA). Appreciative Advising is a research-based strategy to help schools deliver the best quality of education for students to succeed.

AA's framework comprises of six phases: Disarm, Discover, Dream, Design, Deliver and Don't Settle. Disarm involves making a positive first impression with students and allaying any fear or suspicion they might have of meeting with the advisor. Discover is spent continuing to build rapport with students and learning about their strengths, skills and abilities. Dream involves uncovering students' hopes and dreams for their future. Design co-creates a plan for helping students accomplish their dreams. Deliver is the implementation phase where students carry out their plan, and the advisor's role is to support them as they encounter roadblocks. Don't Settle involves challenging the students to achieve their full potential, according to Jennifer Bloom a clinical professor at the University of South Carolina (The Holmes Education Post, 2005).

Another way to cultivate meaningful relations with students while fostering a positive learning environment is to utilize the training toolkit on bullying in the classroom by the U.S. Department of Education. This toolkit comprises of two modules designed to help teachers (1) identify and efficiently intervene when bullying occurs in the educational environment and (2) use effective strategies to build a classroom climate where bullying is less likely to occur in the environment.

Step IX - Evaluate Strategies

Bullying is similar to a cancer. In order to end it, you have to determine the cause for the problem, provide the appropriate interventions or strategies and then monitor the effectiveness of the strategies to determine if the problem is resolved. In the first eight steps of the model, we discussed the plan for eradicating bullying from the school culture. Step IX of the model is to evaluate periodically the anti-bullying prevention strategies at the school.

While many schools use a variety of bullying prevention programs to address the dangers of bullying, there is insufficient research on the evaluation of these programs. According to research, "there is little data to support accurate data collection procedures, well validated outcome measures, and procedures to ensure consistent program implementation" (Leff, Power, Manz, Costigan, & Nabors cited in Wood, 2013).

As such, we propose concepts of the Malcolm Baldrige Model (See, Plan, Do, Check). While using this model in a previous educational setting, it required us to (1) "See" or assess what the needs are in the educational environment; (2)"Plan" appropriately the goals in line with the needs or assessment of the environment; (3) "Do" or carryout the necessary activities to meet the goals and (4) "Check" or evaluate the activities to determine if the goals were met. Figure 10 provides an illustration of this model to evaluate the nine strategies mentioned in this book to eradicate bullying from the school culture. For effectiveness, schools must establish an anti-bullying committee to work closely with the appropriate school officials. Because bullying is deeply rooted in the American culture, schools should consider hiring the necessary support staff such as an anti-bullying coordinator who reports directly to the building principal.

Figure 10.
Evaluate Strategies of Model

See	Assess the school and community environments and understand the meaning of bullying from a historical, psychological, social-ecological and legal perspective
Plan	Educate stakeholders; review policies, procedures and laws; address accountability; discuss the characteristics and signs of bullying; implement activities; communicate impact; adopt best practices; and teach anti-bullying curriculum
Do	Incorporate the Nine Steps of the model and other research-based anti-bullying prevention activities
Check	Evaluate periodically the Nine Steps of the model and other research-based anti-bullying prevention activities.

RESOURCES

The Holmes Education Post, an education focused Internet newspaper that provides information on improving education. The website address is: theholmeseducationpost.com. What can you find on this site?

- *Educational articles to support students, parents, teachers, school administrators, professors and college administrators*
- *Ideas and educational best practices*
- *Listing of high school, undergraduate and graduate scholarships*
- *Videotapes of classroom lectures that demonstrates teaching methods such as Whole Brain Instruction*
- *Recordings of talk shows on various educational topics*
- *Books that focus on improving education*
- *Pilot Online National Anti-Hazing Curriculum for educational institutions*
- *Pilot Online National Anti-Bullying Curriculum for public & private school systems*

Anti-Bullying Alliance – http://www.anti-bullyingalliance.org.uk/
Mission: The Anti-bullying Alliance is a coalition of organizations and individuals working together to stop bullying and create safe environments in which children and young people can live, grow, play and learn.

BullyPolice.org – http://www.bullypolice.org/
Mission: A watch-dog organization that advocates for bullied children and reports on State Anti Bullying Laws.

Bullying.org – http://www.bullying.org/
Mission: Bullying.org is dedicated to increasing the awareness of bullying and to preventing, resolving and eliminating bullying in society.

Center for Parent Information and Resources (CPIR)
http://www.parentcenterhub.org/about-us/
> Mission: CPIR serves as a central resource of information and products to the community of Parent Training Information Centers and the Community Parent Resource Centers, so that they can focus their efforts on serving families of children with disabilities.

Einestine Technology Services (ETS) provides Information Technology training and certification for hardware and software programs such as Microsoft, CISCO, CompTIA Adobe and VmWare to individuals, businesses, as well as local, state and federal agencies — all in a professional, responsive and results oriented manner. ETS also utilizes the latest technologies to deliver a versatile e-learning product custom-designed for its clients.

ETS (www.einestinetechnology.com) offers various formats of e-learning to clients from Live One-to-One training sessions using the latest whiteboard technology, web based trainings, computer based trainings, and ETS Private Network Systems. ETS leverage the latest technologies to deliver all of its trainings which eliminates travel, provides learning based upon clients' needs and gives them total control of their education schedule.

Because of the psychological and physical effects of hazing and bullying, ETS form partnership with The Holmes Education Post to create both an Online National Anti-Hazing Curriculum and Online National Anti-Bullying Curriculum.

Josephson Institute
https://charactercounts.org/resources/youthviolence/
> Mission: To improve the ethical quality of society by changing personal and organizational decision making and behavior.

National Association of School Psychologists
www.nasponline.org/resources/bullying/
> Mission – National Association of School Psychologists empowers school psychologists by advancing effective practices to improve students' learning, behavior, and mental health.

National Education Association
http://www.nea.org/home/neabullyfree.html
> Mission – The National Education Association (NEA) is the nation's largest professional employee organization committed to advancing the cause of public education. NEA's 3 million members work at every level of education—from pre-school to university graduate programs.

Olweus Bullying Prevention Program (OBPP)
http://www.violencepreventionworks.org/public/index.page
> OBPP is a whole-school program that has been proven to prevent or reduce bullying throughout a school setting with over thirty-five years of research and successful implementation all over the world.

Pacer's National Bullying Prevention Center
http://www.pacer.org/bullying/about/
> Mission: Founded in 2006, PACER's National Bullying Prevention Center actively leads social change, so that bullying is no longer considered an accepted childhood rite of passage. PACER provides innovative resources for students, parents, educators, and others, and recognizes bullying as a serious community issue that impacts education, physical and emotional health, and the safety and well-being of students.

Public Justice
http://publicjustice.net/what-we-do/anti-bullying-campaign
> When schools fail to protect children and take appropriate steps to respond to bullying, Public Justice's Anti-Bullying Campaign is designed to hold schools accountable.

Stand for the Silent – http://www.standforthesilent.org/

Stand for the Silent was started in 2010 by a group of students from the Oklahoma State University – Oklahoma City Upward Bound Chapter after they heard the story of Kirk and Laura Smalley's son, Ty Field-Smalley. At eleven years-old, Ty took his own life after being suspended from school for retaliating against a bully that had been bullying him for over two years. Stand for the Silent exist as a platform to allow Kirk and Laura to share their story and offer education and tools that will prevent their tragedy from happening to another child and family. Kirk and Laura's mission is to continue to change kids' lives and bring awareness to bullying and the real devastation it causes.

StompOutBullying.org – http://www.stompoutbullying.org/

Mission: StompOutBullying.org focuses on reducing and preventing bullying, sexting, cyberbullying, and other digital abuse, educating against homophobia, hatred and racism, decreasing absenteeism at school, and deterring violence online, in schools and communities across the nation.

Stopbullying.gov – http://www.stopbullying.gov/

Mission: StopBullying.gov provides information from various government agencies on what bullying is, what cyberbullying is, who is at risk, and how you can prevent and respond to bullying.

The Bully Project – http://www.thebullyproject.com/

Since the release of Bully, the film has been screened to over a million kids, teachers, parents, and advocates. The mission is to build a national movement to end bullying.

Teaching Tolerance – http://www.tolerance.org/about

Mission: Founded in 1991 by the Southern Poverty Law Center, Teaching Tolerance is dedicated to reducing prejudice, improving intergroup relations and supporting equitable school experiences for our nation's children.

REFERENCES

Addressing the problem of juvenile bullying (2001). Retrieved March 30, 2011, fromU.S. Department of Justice, Office of Justice Programs: http://www.ncjrs.gov/Pdffiles1lojjdplfs200127.pdf

Bank, E.J. (2011). Elementary and Middle School Bullying: A Delphi analysis of successful prevention programming. Retrieved from ProQuest (86076112)

Behavioral Management. Bullying Statistics. Retrieved March 30, 2011, from Behavioral Management: http://behavior-management.com/bulling-statistics

BullyPolice.org. Programs that work. Retrieved April 2, 2015, from http://www.bullypolice.org/program.html

Bullying Statistics. Stop bullying now review. Retrieved April 2, 2015, from http://www.bullyingstatistics.org/content/stop-bullying-now-review.html

Bullying Statistics. Retrieved March 30, 2011, from Behavioral Management: http://behavior-management.com/bulling-statistics

Chang, Glenna C. (2011). The hidden curriculum: Hazing and professional identify. Doctoral Dissertation. Retrieved from ProQuest (757558751).

DINatale, V. (2014, September 8). Dept. of Education launches new anti-bullying tools. Retrieved April 2, 2015 from, http://savannahnow.com/accent/2014-09-08/bullying-breakdown-department-education-launches-new-anti-bullying-tools

Education Law Center. Retrieved March 30, 2011, from htt://www.edlawcenter.org/issues/bullying.html

Fegenbush, B. M. (2010). *Comprehensive anti-bullying programs and policies: Using student perceptions to explore the relationships between school-based proactive and reactive measures and acts of bullying on Louisiana High School Campuses. Doctoral dissertation. Retrieved from ProQuest (506439312).*

Hirsch, L. (2012). *The Bully Project. Retrieved October 28, 2013 from, http://www.thebullyproject.com/*

Holmes, R.W. (2011). *Education Questions to be Answered. Bloomington, IN: AuthorHouse.*

Holmes, R.W. (2012). *Current Issues and Answers in Education. Bloomington, IN: AuthorHouse.*

Institute on Family & Neighborhood Life. *Fact Sheet. Retrieved April 2, 2015, fromhttp://www.spannj.org/pti/Fact_Sheet_on_Bullying_Harassment_&_Prevention.pdf*

iSAFE (2012). *Cyber Bullying: Statistics and Tips. Retrieved October 28, 2013 from,http://www.isafe.org/outreach/media/media_cyber_bullying*

Martin and LaVAn (2010). *Workplace bullying: A review of litigated cases. Retrieved April 2, 2015, from https://www.sc.edu/ombuds/doc/Martin_and_LaVan_2010.pdf*

McCormac, M.E. (2015). *Preventing and responding to bullying: An elementary School's 4-year journey. Professional School Counseling. Retrieved April 2, 2015, from http://professionalschoolcounseling.org/toc/prsc/current*

National Education Association (2010). *Retrieved April 2, 2015, from http://www.nea.org/*

National bullying prevention awareness week (2006). *Retrieved March 30, 2011 National Education Association: http://www.pacerkidsagainstbullying.org/NBPAW/parents.asp*

President Obama & the First Lady at the White House conference on bullying prevention (2011). *Retrieved March 30, 2011, from The White House: http://www.whitehouse.gov/search/site/Bullying*

Stopbullying.gov. Key components in Anti-Bullying Laws. Retrieved April, 2, 2015, from http://www.stopbullying.gov/laws/keycomponents/index. html

Stopbullying.gov. Risk factors. Retrieved April 2, 2015, from http://www. stopbullying.gov/at-risk/factors/index.html

Stopbullying.gov. Warning Signs. Retrieved April 2, 2015, from httpp://www. stopbullying.gov/at-risk/warning-signs/index.html

Study.com. Retrieved April 2, 2015 from http://study.com/academy/ lesson/bronfenbrenners-ecological-systems-theory-of-development-definition-examples.html

The Holmes Education Post (2015). What is the aim of Appreciative Advising? Retrieved April 2, 2015 fromhttp://theholmeseducationpost. com/2015/01/what-is-the-aim-of-appreciative-advising/

The Holmes Education Post (2012). Is it time to stand for the silent? Retrieved April 2, 2015 from http://theholmeseducationpost.com/2012/05/ is-it-time-to-"stand-for-the-silent"/

The Holmes Education Post (2014). What is a truancy initiative to keep students in school. Retrieved April 2, 2015 from http://the holmeseducationpost. com2014/10/what-is-a-truancy-initiative-to-keep-students-in-school/

U.S. Department of Education (2012). Giving teachers tools to stop bullying. Free training toolkit. Retrieved April 2, 2015 from http://www.ed.gov/ blog/2012/10/giving-teachers-tools-to-stop-bullying-free-training-toolkit-now- available/

Wood, B. F. (2013). An evaluation of the implementation fidelity and outcomes of the Olweus Prevention Program in three elementary schools in Virginia. Doctoral dissertation. Retrieved from Proquest (1321501134).

AUTHOR'S BACKGROUND

Ronald Holmes is president and publisher
of The Holmes Education Post, an education
focused Internet newspaper. He publishes
weekly articles on educational issues and
offers unique, researched based solutions,
perspectives, best practices, and resources to
improve public education.

Ronald Holmes earned a PhD in Educational
Leadership, a MED in Educational
Administration and Supervision and a BS
in Business Education from Florida A&M
University. He also earned a MED in Business
Education from Bowling Green State University.
He is a former teacher, school administrator,
and district superintendent.

Made in the USA
Middletown, DE
08 January 2016